CONTENTS

Words written in bold, **like this**, are explained in the Glossary.

WHAT IS MILK?

All baby **mammals** drink milk in their first weeks of life. Milk is their food. These lambs are drinking their mother's milk.

Food

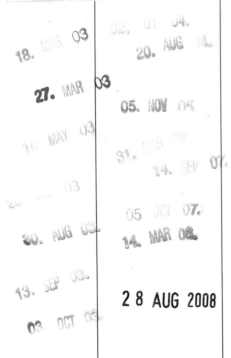

H www.heinemann.co.uk/library
Visit our website to find out more information about Heinemann Library books.

To order:
☎ Phone 44 (0) 1865 888066
🖹 Send a fax to 44 (0) 1865 314091
💻 Visit the Heinemann Bookshop at www.heinemann.co.uk/library to browse our catalogue and order online.

First published in Great Britain by Heinemann Library,
Halley Court, Jordan Hill, Oxford OX2 8EJ
a division of Reed Educational and Professional Publishing Ltd.
Heinemann is a registered trademark of Reed Educational & Professional Publishing Ltd.

OXFORD MELBOURNE AUCKLAND
JOHANNESBURG BLANTYRE GABORONE
IBADAN PORTSMOUTH (NH) USA CHICAGO

© Reed Educational and Professional Publishing Ltd 2002
The moral right of the proprietor has been asserted.

Designed by Celia Floyd
Originated by Ambassador Litho Ltd
Printed by South China Printing Co in Hong Kong.

ISBN 0 431 12701 8 (hardback)   ISBN 0 431 12711 5 (paperback)
05 04 03 02   06 05 04 03 02
10 9 8 7 6 5 4 3 2   10 9 8 7 6 5 4 3 2

British Library Cataloguing in Publication Data
Spilsbury, Louise
  Milk. – (Food)
  1. Milk 2. Cookery (Milk)
  I. Title
  641.3'714

Acknowledgements
The Publishers would like to thank the following for permission to reproduce photographs:
Gareth Boden pp.20, 21, 22, 23, 28, 29; Bridgeman Art Library p.6; Corbis pp.10, /Kevin Fleming p.9, /Richard Hamilton Smith p.14, /Bob Rowan, Progressive Image p.19; FLPA /E & D Hosking p.11; Holt Studios/Nigel Cattlin p.13; National Dairy Council pp.15, 16, 17, 18; Oxford Scientific Films /Paul McCullagh p.8, /Jorge Sierra p.4; Photodisc/Russell Illig p.5; Stock Market p.25; Tony Stone/David Madison p.24, /Graeme Norways p.12, /Catherine Panchout p.7.

Cover photograph reproduced with permission of Gareth Boden.

Every effort has been made to contact copyright holders of any material reproduced in this book. Any omissions will be rectified in subsequent printings if notice is given to the Publisher.

People drink milk from other mammals, such as cows, sheep and goats. The milk that most people drink comes from cows.

IN THE PAST

In the past, some **bacteria** in milk made people ill. About 140 years ago, the French **scientist** Louis Pasteur found that heating milk killed off the harmful bacteria.

This **process** is known as **pasteurization.** It was named after Pasteur. Pasteurization is still used today to make sure our milk is safe to drink.

AROUND THE WORLD

Cows cannot live in the high, cold mountains of the **Himalayas**. People there keep **yaks** for their milk. They also make butter and cheese from yak milk.

In some places people keep goats for their milk. This woman in Greece is milking her goat by hand. The milk is for her family to drink.

COWS AND CALVES

Cows make milk when they have a baby. The **calf** drinks the milk from its mother's **udders**. A cow makes milk for ten months after having a calf.

On a **dairy farm** the calf drinks its mother's milk for a few days. Then the farmer gives it other food. Now the farmer can take the cow's milk to sell.

GETTING THE MILK

The milk most of us drink comes from big **dairy farms**. Tubes from machines suck out the milk from the cows' **udders**. Cows may be milked twice a day.

Milk goes **sour** quite quickly. To keep milk fresh, people keep it cold and covered. At the farm, milk is kept in huge, cold **storage tanks**.

WHAT HAPPENS NEXT?

A big road tanker collects the milk. The tanker has a special lining. This keeps the milk cold and fresh until it gets to the **dairy**.

At the dairy, someone tests the milk.
They check that the milk is clean. If
the milk is good, it is unloaded into
large **storage tanks**.

TREATING THE MILK

Next, the milk is **pasteurized**. It is heated up and then cooled down very quickly. This kills off any **bacteria** in the milk that might make us ill.

Then the milk is packed into clean containers. The containers are filled to the top with milk. The tops or lids are sealed tightly.

MILK TO YOU

The containers of milk are loaded onto crates. These crates are stacked in a lorry. The lorry is cold inside, like a fridge. This keeps the milk fresh.

The lorry takes the milk to the shops for **consumers** to buy. The milk you buy probably only takes two days to get from the cow to you.

KINDS OF MILK

Before milk is bottled, it may be **processed** into different kinds of milk, and into cream. Semi-skimmed and skimmed milks have less **fat**. The fat is called cream.

milk   cream

Fresh milk lasts only up to 14 days. Some milk is processed so that it keeps longer. Milk powder keeps for months. You mix it with water to make milk.

USING MILK

Milk can be used in many different ways. You can make hot and cold drinks with it. Milk is also used in cooking to make sauces, soups and pancakes.

Milk is also used to make different **dairy products**. Cheese, cream, butter and yoghurt are made from milk. Milk and cream are used in ice-cream.

GOOD FOR YOU

Milk contains **nutrients** that keep you healthy and give you **energy**. One of these nutrients is **calcium**. This helps your bones and teeth grow strong.

Milk also contains **protein**. Protein gives your body the energy it needs to repair itself and grow.

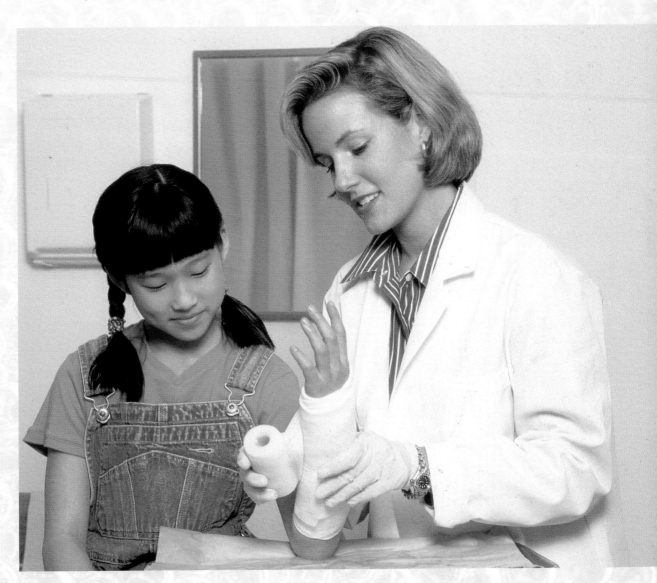

HEALTHY EATING

You need different kinds of food to keep well. This food pyramid shows how much of each different kind of food you need.

The foods in the group at the bottom of the pyramid can be eaten at every meal. You should eat some of the foods shown in the middle every day.

Milk, and foods made from it, are in the middle. Cream has a lot of **fat**, so it belongs in the top of the pyramid. You need only small amounts of the foods at the top.

The foods shown in each part of the pyramid help your body in different ways.

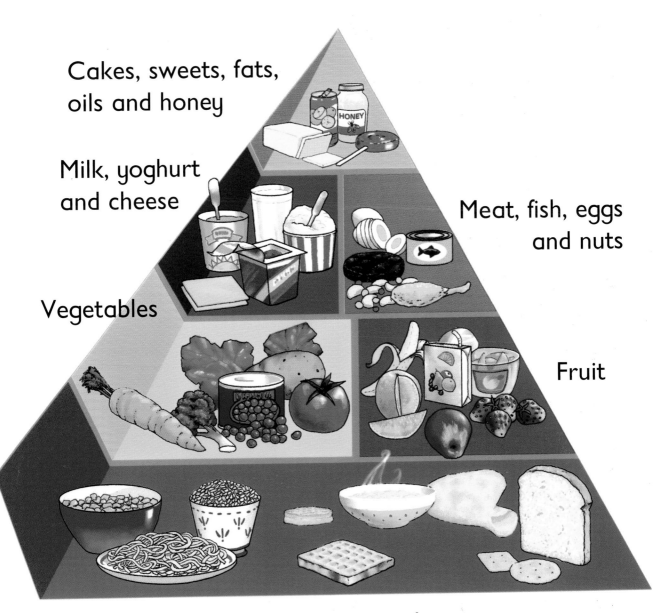

Cakes, sweets, fats, oils and honey

Milk, yoghurt and cheese

Meat, fish, eggs and nuts

Vegetables

Fruit

Bread, **cereals**, rice and pasta

CHOCOLATE MILKSHAKE RECIPE

1 Put the drinking chocolate into a bowl and mix it with hot water to make a paste.

You will need:
- 2 tablespoons drinking chocolate
- 1 tablespoon hot water
- 250 ml cold milk
- 2 small scoops vanilla ice-cream

2 Add cold milk and vanilla ice-cream.

Ask an adult to help you!

28

3 Mix them together with a whisk or an electric blender.

4 Pour the milkshake into a glass. Now it is ready for you to drink.

GLOSSARY

bacteria creatures so small we cannot see them. Some bacteria are harmful and can give us diseases that make us ill.

calcium nutrient that helps to keep our bones and teeth strong and healthy

calf/calves baby cow(s)

consumers people who buy things that they need or want, like food

dairy place where milk and milk products (like cheese and butter) are prepared

dairy farm farm where cows are kept for their milk

dairy products food and drinks made from milk

energy all living things need energy to live, move and grow. Our energy comes from the food we eat.

fat nutrient found in some foods. It is not healthy to eat or drink too much fat.

Himalayas mountains in countries like Nepal and Tibet in Asia

mammals group of animals that includes humans. Mammals feed their young on the mother's milk.

nutrient goodness in food that we need to stay healthy

pasteurization when milk is heated to very high temperatures to kill off any harmful bacteria it might contain

pasteurized see pasteurization (above)

process treat food (or other materials) in a certain way to make something else

processed food that has been treated to make something else

protein nutrient needed to help our bodies form, grow and repair themselves

scientist person who studies the world around us and how it works

sour bad. When milk turns sour it is no longer fresh. It smells and tastes bad.

storage tank large container for holding a liquid, like water or milk

udders where milk is made and stored in cows. Calves suck the milk from teats that are on the ends of the udders.

yak large, long-haired animal like a cow. Yaks' long hair keeps them warm so they can live in cold places.

31

MORE BOOKS TO READ

Farm Animals: Cows, Rachael Bell,
    Heinemann Library, 2000

Safe and Sound: Eat Well, Angela Royston,
    Heinemann Library, 1999

I Know How My Cells Make Me Grow,
    Heinemann Library, 2001

What's for Lunch? Milk, Franklin Watts

Body Works: Eating, Paul Bennet, Belitha Press

INDEX